W9-CFB-608

ALIENS

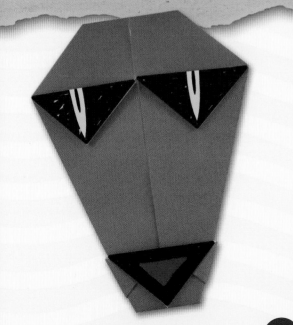

Joe Fullman

Gareth Stevens
PUBLISHING

Please visit our website, www.garethstevens.com. For a free color catalog of all our high-quality books, call toll free 1-800-542-2595 or fax 1-877-542-2596.

Cataloging-in-Publication Data

Names: Fullman, Joe.
Title: Aliens / Joe Fullman.
Description: New York : Gareth Stevens Publishing, 2020. | Series: Amazing Origami | Includes glossary and index.
Identifiers: ISBN 9781538242339 (pbk.) | ISBN 9781538241790 (library bound) | ISBN 9781538242346 (6 pack)
Subjects: LCSH: Origami–Juvenile literature. | Extraterrestrial beings in art–Juvenile literature.
Classification: LCC TT872.5 F85 2019 | DDC 736'.982–dc23

First Edition

Published in 2020 by
Gareth Stevens Publishing
111 East 14th Street, Suite 349
New York, NY 10003

Models created by Picnic
Photography by Michael Wilkes
Text by Joe Fullman
Design by Emma Randall

Printed in the United States of America

CPSIA compliance information: Batch #CW20GS: For further information contact Gareth Stevens, New York, New York at 1-800-542-2595.

CoNTENTS

Introduction...................................... 4

Getting Started 5

Alien 8

UFO..12

Martian...16

Pet Robot..18

Neptunian 20

Octopod 24

Glossary 30

Further Information 31

Index 32

INTRODUCTION

AAARGH!

This beastly book will show you how to make an assortment of aliens from other worlds. You'll make origami visitors from Mars, Neptune, and beyond—as well as the craft that brought them here.

In traditional origami, models are made from one sheet of folded paper and there is no cutting involved. We've broken the rules a little, to give our models tentacles, eyes, and other features. Ask an adult to help with any projects that need scissors. Otherwise, all you need to get you started is a square of paper and your fingers. If you haven't made origami models before, try some of the easy projects first. Now get ready for some fiendish folding!

BEEP BEEP!!

GETTING STARTED

The paper used in origami is thin but strong, so that it can be folded many times. You can use ordinary scrap paper, as long as it's not too thick.

A lot of the origami models in this book are made with the same folds. This introduction explains some of the ones that will appear most, so it's a good idea to master these folds before you start. When making the projects, follow the key below to find out what the lines and arrows mean. And always crease well!

KEY

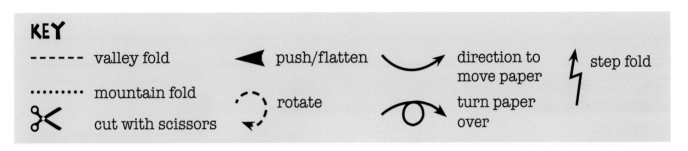

- – – – – – valley fold
- ·········· mountain fold
- ✂ cut with scissors
- ◀ push/flatten
- ◌ rotate
- ⤳ direction to move paper
- ⟲ turn paper over
- ↯ step fold

VALLEY FOLD

To make a valley fold, fold the paper toward you, so that the crease is pointing away from you, like a valley.

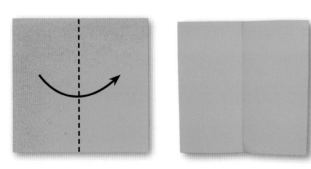

MOUNTAIN FOLD

To make a mountain fold, fold the paper the other way so the crease is pointing up toward you, like a mountain.

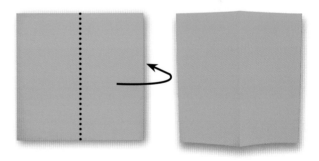

STEP FOLD

A step fold is used to make a step or zigzag in the paper. We'll use it to make ears, tails, and other monstrous features.

1 Valley fold the paper in half. Then make a mountain fold directly above the valley fold.

2 Push the mountain fold down over the valley fold and press down flat.

3 You now have a step fold. You can also make it in reverse, with the mountain fold first.

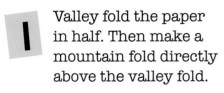

This is a useful fold if you want to flatten part of an origami model. It's a good way to create tails and snouts for your alien creations.

 Fold a piece of paper diagonally in half. Make a valley fold on one corner and crease.

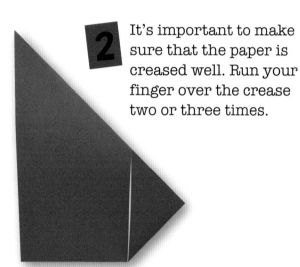

2 It's important to make sure that the paper is creased well. Run your finger over the crease two or three times.

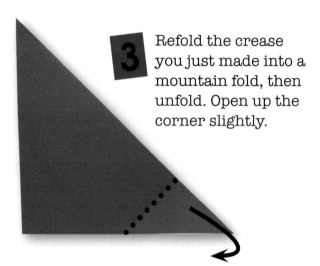

3 Refold the crease you just made into a mountain fold, then unfold. Open up the corner slightly.

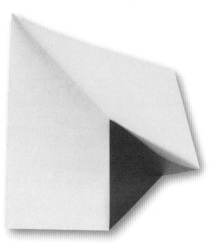

4 Open up the paper a little more and then tuck the tip of the corner inside. Close the paper. This is the view from the underside of the paper.

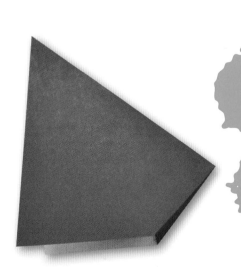

5 Flatten the paper. You now have an inside reverse fold.

OUTSIDE REVERSE FOLD

This is great if you want to make part of your model stick out. It will come in handy for making heads.

1 Fold a piece of paper diagonally in half. Make a valley fold on one corner and crease.

2 It's important to make sure that the paper is creased well. Run your finger over the crease two or three times.

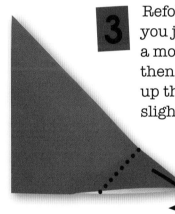

3 Refold the crease you just made into a mountain fold, then unfold. Open up the corner slightly.

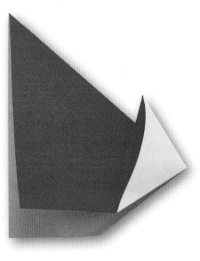

4 Open up the paper a little more and start to turn the corner inside out. Then close the paper when the fold begins to turn.

5 You now have an outside reverse fold. You can either flatten the paper or leave it rounded out.

7

ALIEN

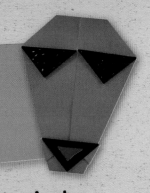

Do you believe in aliens? Making this project may just convince you. It's out of this world!

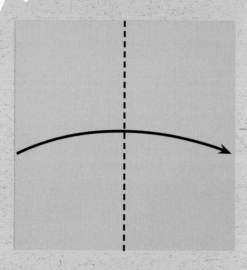

1 Place your paper like this, white side up. Fold it in half from left to right, then unfold.

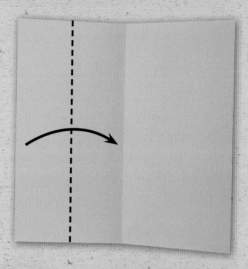

2 Fold the left-hand edge over to the middle crease.

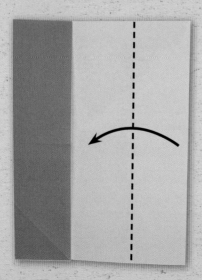

3 Fold the right-hand edge over to the middle crease.

4 Fold the top point of the upper layer across to the left edge.

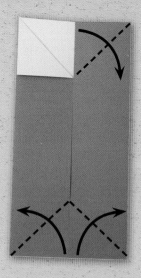

5

Repeat Step 4 with the other three corners.

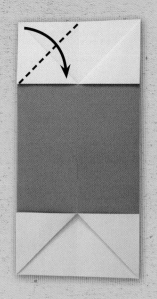

6

Fold the top left point over to the middle crease.

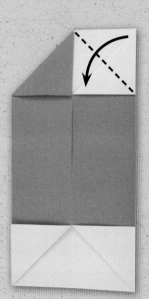

7

Fold the top right point over to the middle crease.

UNFOLD   UNFOLD

8

Open out the folds you made in Steps 6 and 7.

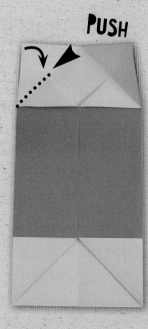

PUSH

9

Bring the top left point over to the middle crease again. As you do, push up the fold that's been highlighted from below so that it becomes a mountain fold.

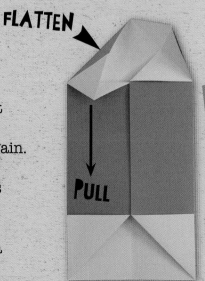

FLATTEN

PULL

10

Pull the point of the mountain fold down, as shown. Flatten it down. This is your alien's first eye.

11

Your paper should look like this. Repeat Steps 9 and 10 on the right-hand side.

12

Mountain fold the top point over and behind.

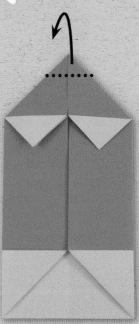

13

Fold up the bottom edge, as shown, to create a new flap.

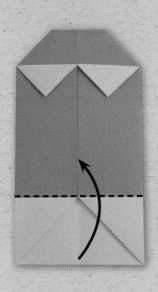

14

Fold the top left point of the new flap down to the bottom edge.

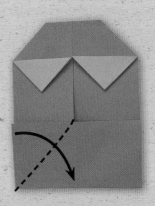

15

Repeat Step 14 on the right-hand side.

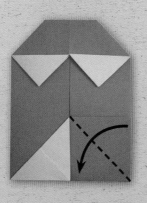

16

Fold up the left point of the upper layer, as shown.

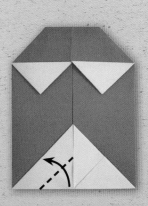

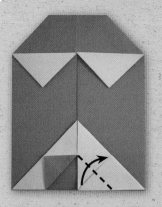

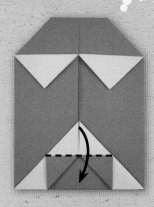

17

Repeat Step 16 on the right-hand side.

18

Fold the middle point over and down so it touches the bottom edge.

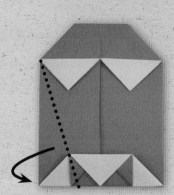

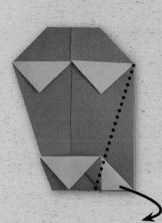

19

Mountain fold the left-hand side of the paper at an angle.

20

Repeat Step 19 on the right-hand side.

21

Add some spooky-looking eyes and your alien is ready to board its spaceship.

TAKE ME TO YOUR LEADER!

UF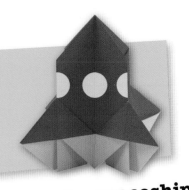

If aliens want to visit Earth, they'll need a spaceship to travel in—just like this one. 3, 2, 1 ... liftoff!

TURN OVER

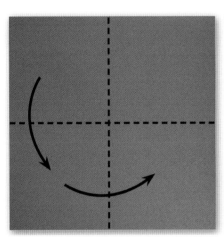

1 Place your paper white side down with a straight edge facing you. Valley fold it in half from top to bottom, and unfold. Then valley fold it in half from left to right, and unfold.

2 Turn the paper over from left to right.

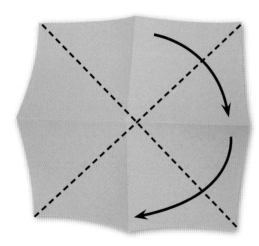

3 Fold the top-left corner to the bottom right, and unfold. Then fold the top right corner down to the bottom left, and unfold.

PUSH ▶ 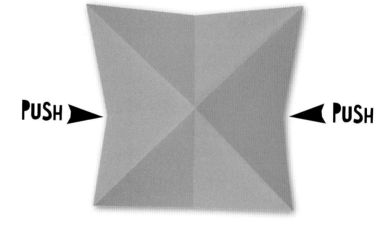 **◀ PUSH**

4 Push the left- and right-hand edges in toward each other.

▼ PRESS

5 As you push, the paper should start folding in on itself, forming a triangle shape. Press it down flat.

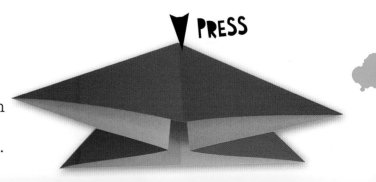

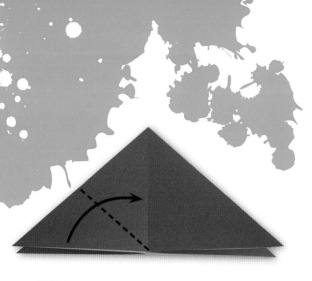

6 Your paper should look like this. Fold the bottom left point of the upper layer up to the top.

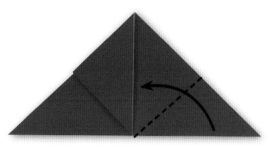

7 Repeat Step 6 on the right-hand side.

OPEN

8 Open up the flap you made in Step 7 so it forms a mouthlike shape.

FLATTEN

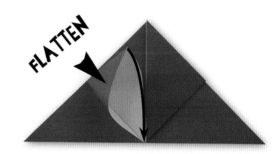

9 Bring the top point down and flatten the flap down so it forms a square shape.

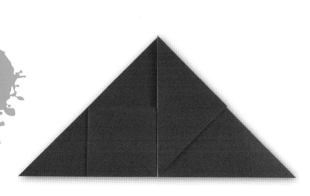

10 Your paper should look like this. Repeat Steps 8 and 9 on the right-hand side.

TURN OVER

11 Turn the paper over from left to right.

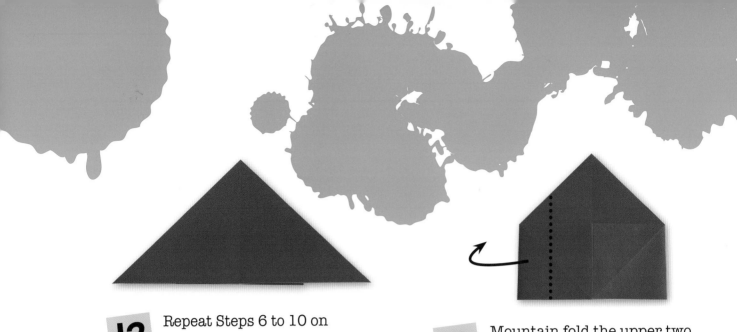

12 Repeat Steps 6 to 10 on this side.

13 Mountain fold the upper two left-hand layers in half.

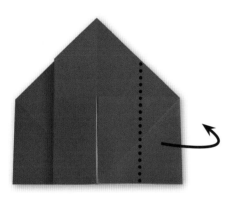

14 Your paper should look like this, with just the upper two layers folded under. Repeat Step 13 on the right-hand side.

15 Make a small fold to the bottom edge of the upper layer on the left-hand side.

16 Repeat Step 15 on the right-hand side.

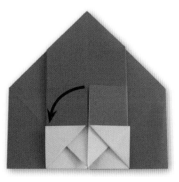

17 Open up the left-hand flap and pull the top point down and to the left.

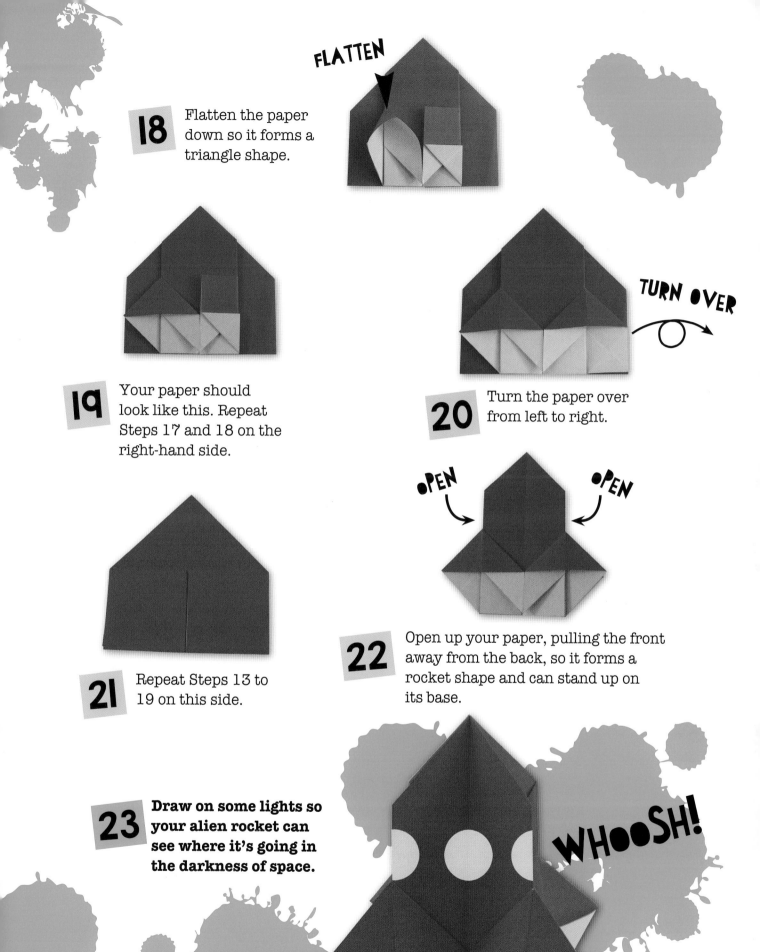

FLATTEN

18 Flatten the paper down so it forms a triangle shape.

19 Your paper should look like this. Repeat Steps 17 and 18 on the right-hand side.

TURN OVER

20 Turn the paper over from left to right.

OPEN **OPEN**

21 Repeat Steps 13 to 19 on this side.

22 Open up your paper, pulling the front away from the back, so it forms a rocket shape and can stand up on its base.

23 Draw on some lights so your alien rocket can see where it's going in the darkness of space.

WHOOSH!

MARTIAN

Some people think there are little green men living on Mars. How wrong can they be? They're obviously bright scarlet. They're from the Red Planet, after all.

1 Place your paper like this, white side up, with a corner facing you. Fold it in half from left to right, then unfold.

2 Fold the left and right top edges to the middle crease, as shown.

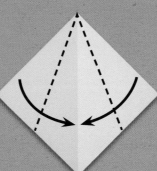

3 Mountain fold the bottom white triangle behind.

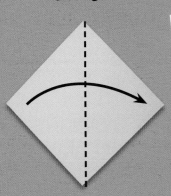

4 Fold the top point down, as shown, leaving a small triangle at the top of the paper.

5 Your paper should look like this. Turn it over from left to right.

TURN OVER

6 Fold the top point down, as shown.

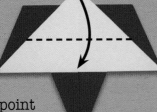

7 Make two small folds in the bottom two points, so that the bottom point touches the lower edge of the higher fold.

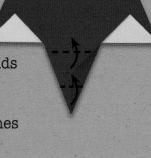

8 Unfold the bottom fold you made in Step 7.

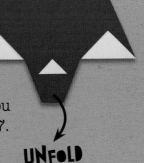

UNFOLD

q Open out the fold at the sides.

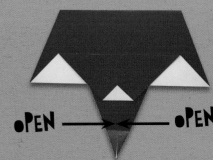

OPEN ——▶ ◀—— OPEN

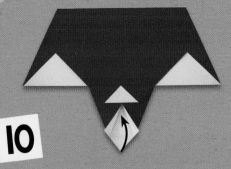

10 Lift the bottom point up and flatten it down.

11 Your paper should look like this. Fold the bottom point of the upper layer down.

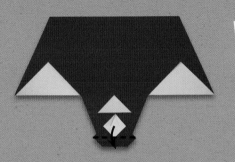

12 Fold the edge over again, as shown.

13 Fold the top left-hand and top right-hand corners over to form two new flaps.

14 Make a fold in the left-hand flap you made in Step 13.

15 Make another fold halfway along the fold you made in Step 14, but only push it a little way back.

16 Repeat Steps 14 and 15 on the right-hand side.

17 Add some scary features and your Martian is "red"-y!

PET RoBoT

Just as we have cats and dogs, aliens have their own pet robots. Follow these steps to make a pet robot of your own.

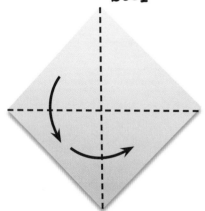

1 Place your paper white side down with a corner facing you. Valley fold it in half from top to bottom, and unfold. Then valley fold it in half from left to right, and unfold.

2 Fold the bottom corner up to the middle crease.

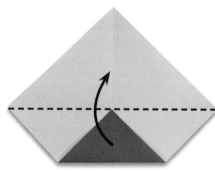

TURN OVER

3 Fold up the bottom edge along the middle crease.

4 Turn the paper over from left to right.

5 Fold the left-hand point over to the right, as shown.

6 Fold the triangle-shaped flap you made in Step 5 in half from bottom to top, so it forms a new flap.

7 Fold the top point of the flap you just made down and to the left.

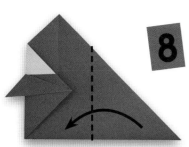

8 Valley fold the right-hand point all the way over to the left to form a new triangle-shaped flap.

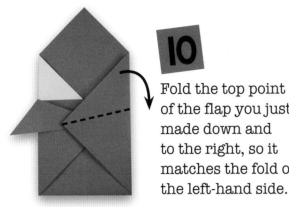

9 Fold the new triangle-shaped flap in half from bottom to top.

10 Fold the top point of the flap you just made down and to the right, so it matches the fold on the left-hand side.

11 Fold the top point down so it fits within the two white triangles on either side.

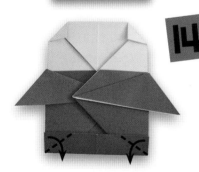

12 Fold down the top points on either side, as shown.

13 Fold up a small strip at the bottom of the paper.

Make two angled folds at either end of the strip, as shown. **14**

15 Your paper should look like this. Turn it over from left to right.

TURN OVER

16 Add some eyes and some buttons. It's time to switch on your pet robot!

BEEEP!

BEEEP!

NEPTUNIAN

This strange-looking creature is from Neptune—the planet farthest from the sun in the solar system. It's so far away, and so dark, that the alien needs three eyes to see!

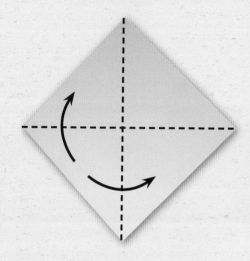

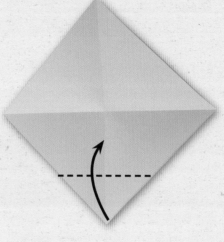

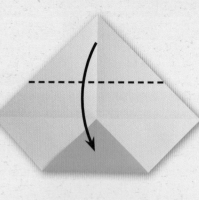

1 Place your paper like this, white side up, with a corner facing you. Fold it in half from left to right, and unfold. Then fold it from bottom to top, and unfold.

2 Fold the bottom point up to the middle crease.

3 Fold the top point down to the bottom edge.

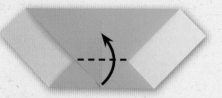

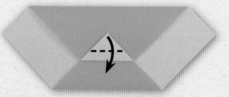

4 Fold the bottom point up, as show.

5 Fold the middle point over, as shown.

6 Fold the middle point up to form a white triangle, a bit lower than the white triangles on either side.

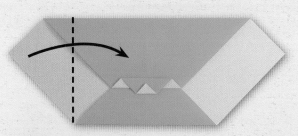

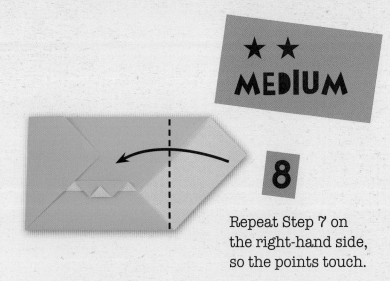

7 Fold the left-hand point over to the middle.

8 Repeat Step 7 on the right-hand side, so the points touch.

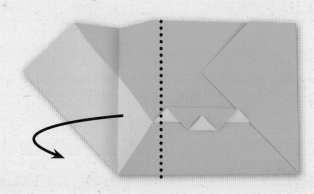

UNFOLD

9 Unfold the fold you made in Step 7.

10 Mountain fold the left-hand side of the paper so the crease you made in Step 7 lines up with the middle crease at the back of the paper. Keep the left-hand point facing left, so it sticks out from behind the paper.

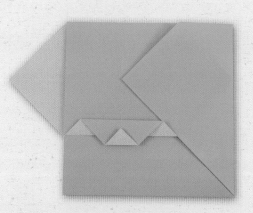

TURN OVER

11 Repeat Steps 9 and 10 on the right-hand side.

12 Your paper should look like this. Turn it over from left to right.

OPEN

PULL FLATTEN

13 Open up the upper two layers of paper in the top left-hand corner.

14 Pull the left central point out and over to the left so it begins to form a triangle shape. Flatten it down.

15 Repeat Steps 13 and 14 on the right-hand side.

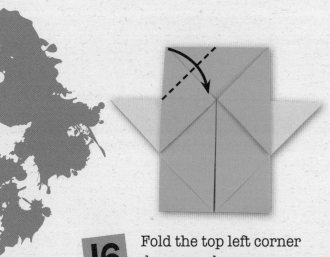

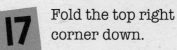

16 Fold the top left corner down, as shown.

17 Fold the top right corner down.

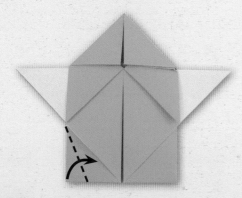

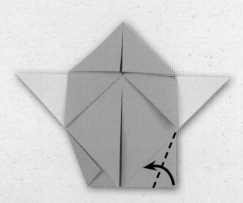

18 Fold the bottom left corner up so it lines up with the diagonal edge above it.

19 Fold the bottom right corner up.

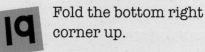

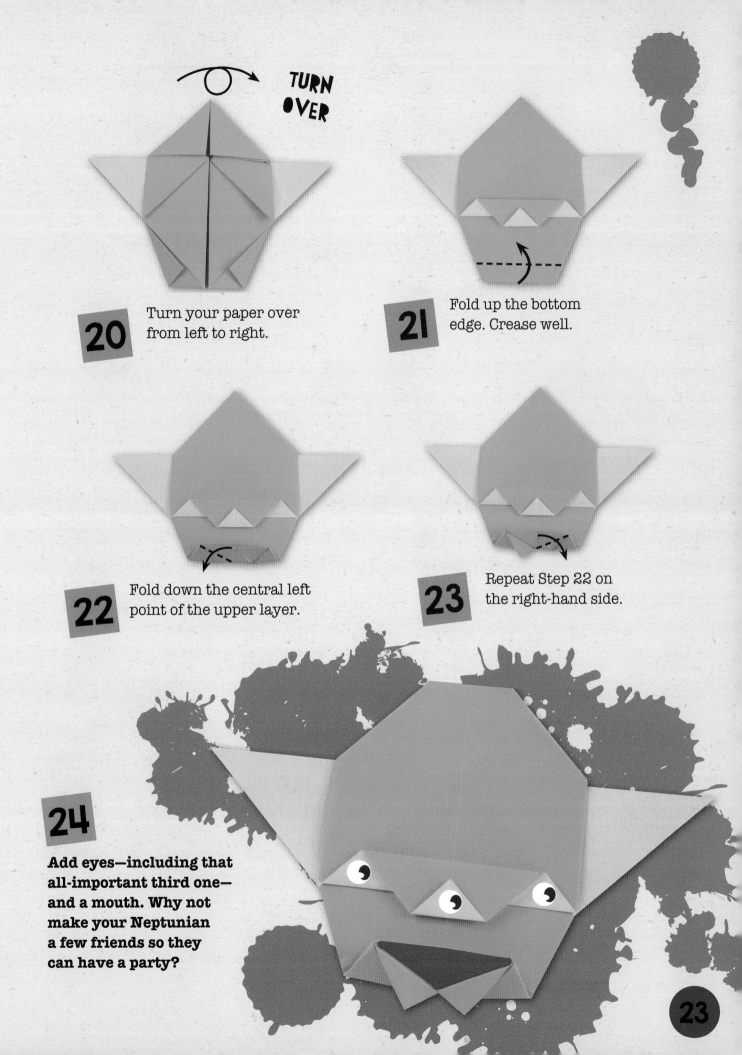

TURN OVER

20 Turn your paper over from left to right.

21 Fold up the bottom edge. Crease well.

22 Fold down the central left point of the upper layer.

23 Repeat Step 22 on the right-hand side.

24

Add eyes—including that all-important third one—and a mouth. Why not make your Neptunian a few friends so they can have a party?

OCTOPOD

Be careful if you visit the planet where this scary creature lives, as it might try to grab you with its long tentacles. You'll need scissors to complete this project.

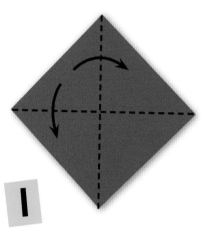

1

Place your paper like this, white side down, with a corner facing you. Fold it in half from left to right, and unfold. Then fold it from top to bottom, and unfold.

TURN OVER

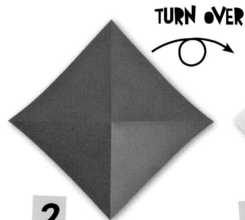

2

Turn the paper over from left to right.

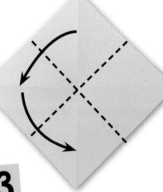

3

Fold the top right edge down to the bottom, and unfold. Then fold the top left edge down to the bottom, and unfold.

PUSH **PUSH**

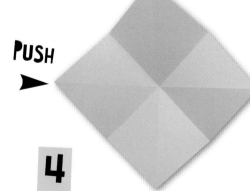

4

Start pushing the left and right corners in toward each other.

FLATTEN

5

As you push, the paper should start folding up into a small square like this. Flatten it down.

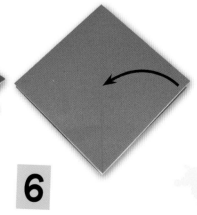

6

Bring the right point of the upper layer over to the middle.

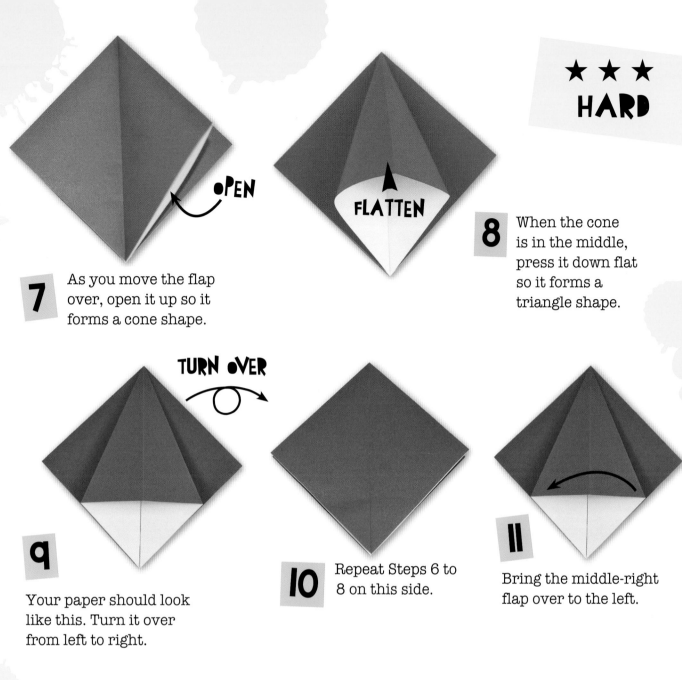

OPEN

FLATTEN

7 As you move the flap over, open it up so it forms a cone shape.

8 When the cone is in the middle, press it down flat so it forms a triangle shape.

TURN OVER

9 Your paper should look like this. Turn it over from left to right.

10 Repeat Steps 6 to 8 on this side.

11 Bring the middle-right flap over to the left.

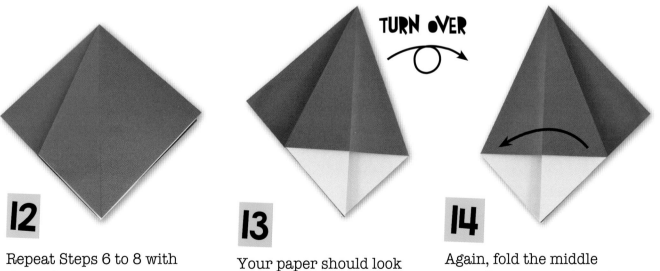

12 Repeat Steps 6 to 8 with the right point.

13 Your paper should look like this. Turn it over from left to right.

TURN OVER

14 Again, fold the middle right flap over to the left.

15

For the final time, repeat Steps 6 to 8 with the right point.

16

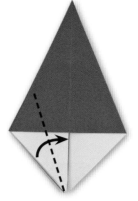

Your paper should look this, with a point at the top and two sets of pointy flaps at the bottom. Fold the bottom-left edge of the upper layer over to the middle crease.

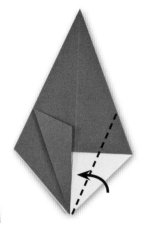

17

Fold the right-hand point of the upper layer over to the middle.

UNFOLD   UNFOLD

18

Unfold the folds you made in Steps 16 and 17.

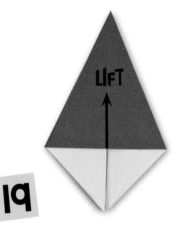

LIFT

19

Lift the bottom edge of the triangle-shaped flap up toward the top. As you do, the folds you made in Steps 16 and 17 should start coming together to form a shape like a bird's mouth.

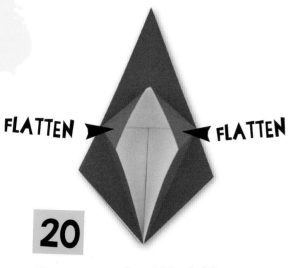

FLATTEN ▶   ◀ **FLATTEN**

20

Your paper should look like this. Flatten the sides down.

TURN OVER

21

Turn the paper over from left to right.

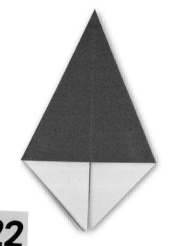

22

Repeat Steps 16 to 20 on this side.

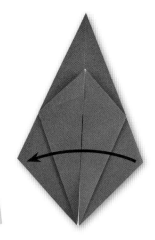

23

Bring the far right-hand point of the upper layer over to the left.

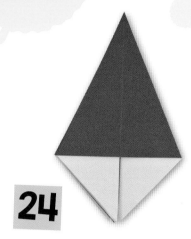

24

Repeat Steps 16 to 20 on this side.

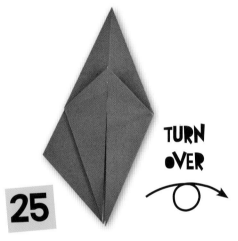

TURN OVER

25

Turn your paper over from left to right.

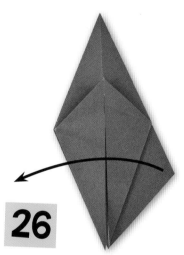

26

Again, fold the right-hand corner of the upper layer over to the left.

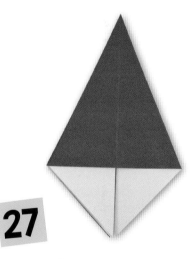

27

For the final time, repeat Steps 16 to 20.

28

Your paper should look like this. Bring the right-hand point of the upper layer over to the left.

TURN OVER

29

Turn the paper over from left to right.

30

Again, bring the right-hand point of the upper layer over to the left.

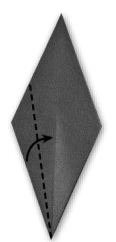

31

Fold the bottom left edge of the upper layer over to the middle.

32

Fold the bottom right edge of the upper layer over to the middle.

33

Repeat Steps 31 and 32 on the other three sides.

34

Your paper should look like this. Fold the bottom point of the upper layer up to the top.

35

Repeat Step 34 on the other three sides. You'll have to open the paper up a little to do this.

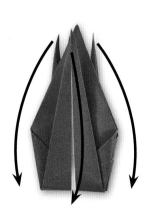

36

Bring the flaps you made in Steps 34 and 35 down so they form the arms of a star shape, as in the image for Step 37.

37 Use your scissors to cut one of the arms in half. These are your first tentacles.

38 Repeat Step 37 with the other three arms to make eight tentacles in total.

39 Inflate the octopod's head by blowing into it from below.

BLOW

40 Place the head and tentacles downward.

41 Your eight-armed octopod is ready to scuttle around its alien world. Use more paper to create a whole octopod alien army.

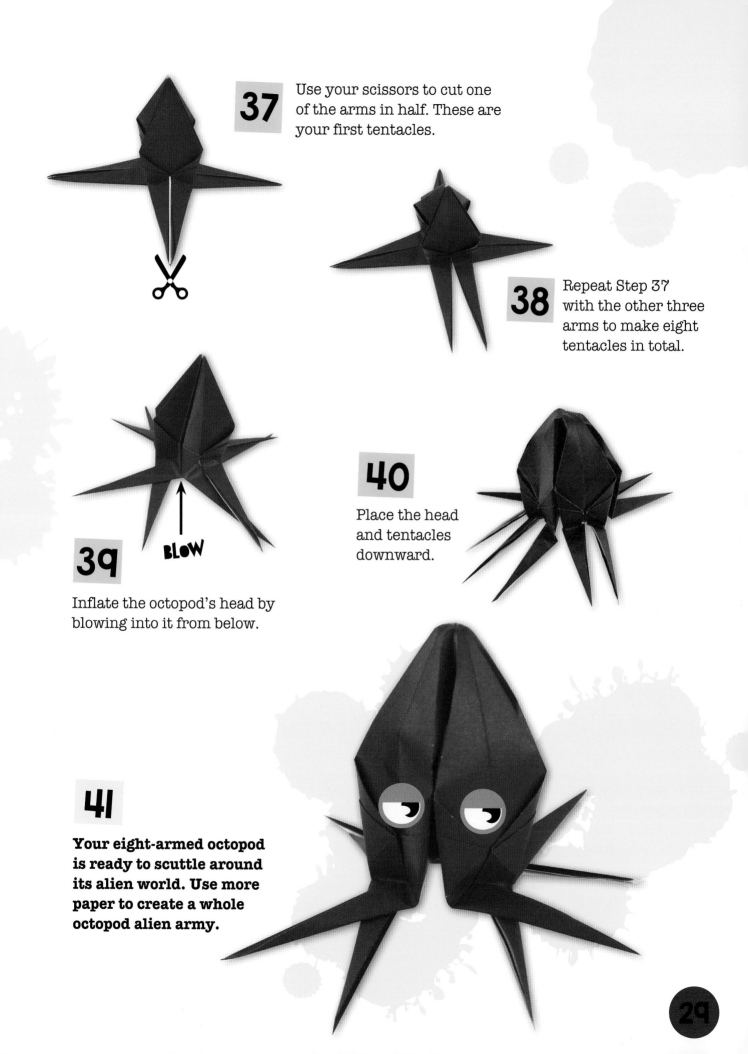

GLOSSARY

crease To fold.

Martian Something from the planet Mars, the fourth planet from the sun in the solar system.

Neptunian Something from the planet Neptune, the farthest planet from the sun in the solar system.

octopod Any animal with eight arms with suckers.

Red Planet Another name for the planet Mars, because its surface contains lots of iron oxide, which makes it look red from space.

robot A machine that acts like a person in being able to move and do complicated actions.

rocket A vehicle powered by the release of gases by combustion.

tentacles Long, thin body parts that project from the heads or bodies of some animals, used for feeling or moving.

UFO Stands for Unidentified Flying Object. A flying object in the sky that some people believe could be a spaceship from another planet.

FURTHER INFORMATION

BOOKS

Dewar, Andrew. *Origami Toy Monsters Kit: Easy-to-Assemble Paper Toys That Shudder, Shake, Lurch and Amaze!* Clarendon, VT: Tuttle Publishing, 2015.

James, Elizabeth. *Easy Origami for Children.* Twickenham, UK: Kyle Craig Publishing, 2017.

Nguyen, Duy. *Tut Monstergami: Paper Folding for Your Inner Monster.* New York, NY: Sterling, 2015.

WEBSITES

https://www.hellowonderful.co/post/diy-origami-paper-monsters/
This website shows you how to make paper monsters that can be used as bookmarks or hand puppets.

https://www.youtube.com/watch?v=YVkJPCp_1UQ
Learn how to make a corner bookmark monster in this video.

Publisher's note to educators and parents: Our editors have carefully reviewed these websites to ensure that they are suitable for students. Many websites change frequently, however, and we cannot guarantee that a site's future contents will continue to meet our high standards of quality and educational value. Be advised that students should be closely supervised whenever they access the internet.

INDEX

arms 29

eyes 9, 11, 19, 23, 29

faces 11, 19, 23, 29
folds
    inside reverse fold 6
    mountain fold 5
    outside reverse fold 7
    step fold 5
    valley fold 5

heads 11, 19, 23, 29

lights 15

Mars 16-19
mouths 11, 23

Neptune 20-23

octopods 24-29

rocket 12-15

spaceship 11, 12-15

tentacles 24, 29

UFOs 12-15